W9-BRE-755

PONTIAC
Chief of the Ottawas

by Jane Fleischer
illustrated by Robert Baxter

Troll Associates

Copyright © 1979 by Troll Associates
All rights reserved. No part of this book may be used or reproduced
in any manner whatsoever without written permission from the publisher.
Printed in the United States of America.

Troll Associates, Mahwah, N.J.

Library of Congress Catalog Card Number: 78-18050
ISBN 0-89375-156-1

PONTIAC

Chief of the Ottawas

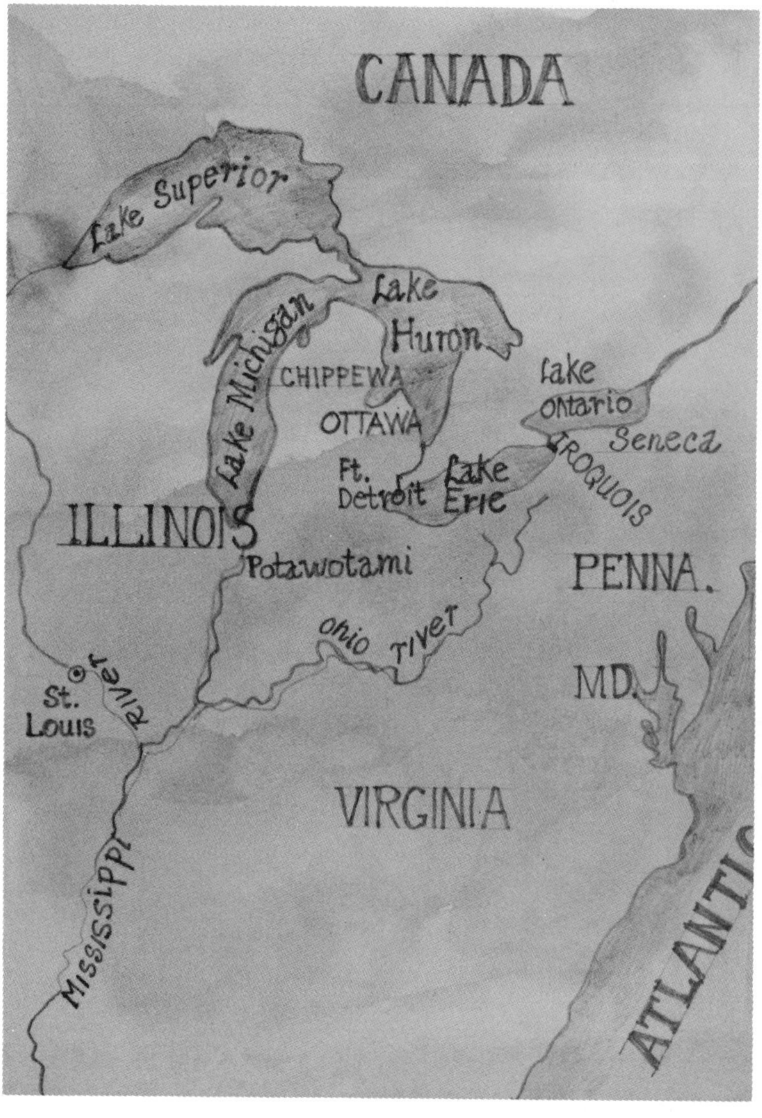
CANADA
Lake Superior
Lake Huron
Lake Michigan
CHIPPEWA
OTTAWA
Lake Ontario
Seneca
Ft. Detroit
Lake Erie
IROQUOIS
ILLINOIS
Potawotami
PENNA.
Ohio river
MD.
St. Louis
River
VIRGINIA
Mississippi
ATLANTI

In a bark-covered cabin, a small Indian baby cried out. This was a special day. Although he had been born many months ago, today he would be given his name.

First, by Ottawa custom, his ears were pierced for beads and his nose pierced for a stone. His people believed the bright stone would keep him safe from danger.

When this was done, the proud father held the child for all to see, declaring, "My son will be called Pontiac."

No one could know that one day this child would lead the warriors of many tribes against the mighty king of England!

Pontiac's people moved with the seasons. In the winter they lived in small tepees in the woodlands of the Great Lakes area. There, each family hunted deer, beavers, bears, otters, raccoons, and other wild game. By spring, their canoes were full of furs for trading.

6

Pontiac's father taught him the ways of the forest. The boy learned to read animal tracks in the snow. He learned to move silently, to wait, to listen, and to aim his arrows straight.

One day he would have a gun like his father's. First, he must learn well. The woods were his school, and he was an eager pupil.

To Pontiac, spring was the best season. He could not wait to enjoy the sweet sap of the maple trees. After a long winter of almost nothing but meat, the maple sugar tasted so good!

He watched as his mother stirred the boiling syrup. Pontiac loved the delicious smell that filled the woods.

But most of all, Pontiac looked forward to late spring, when the Ottawas would take their winter's catch down the river to Fort Detroit. Here the friendly French traders exchanged wonderful gifts for the Indians' furs.

This year, Pontiac felt very grown-up. He had learned to hunt well. He had furs of his own to trade.

As the Ottawas paddled their canoes down the river, Pontiac could see the bright French flag waving above the fort.

His father greeted the Frenchmen as old friends. Many years before, these people had changed the Ottawas' way of life.

The French traders had steel knives and axes that were better than stone tools. Pontiac's mother cooked in brass kettles instead of clay pots. She sewed dresses and shirts of cotton instead of skins.

Most important, the French brought guns and powder, which were far better than bows and arrows for hunting.

Pontiac traded a beaver pelt he had trapped for a bright red blanket. He wore it proudly.

11

All summer, Pontiac's tribe lived across the river from the fort. The long, bark-covered houses of the Ottawas looked something like loaves of bread. Each longhouse was big enough for several families to share.

Early in the spring, Pontiac's mother planted a patch of corn, beans, peas, and pumpkins. In the fall, the corn would be ground for flour, and the other vegetables dried for winter.

Pontiac was allowed to play inside the stockade walls of the village. After the long winter, summer was a happy time for feasts and races and games.

Summer was also a time for war!

Enemy tribes often came to the rich Ottawa hunting grounds. Ottawa warriors would have to fight their enemies and drive them away.

Pontiac grew up to be a tall, strong warrior who showed great courage. Like the other men of his tribe, he wore several feathers tied in his straight black hair. His body was covered with bear grease. During the summer months, he wore little more than moccasins, a breechcloth, beads, and war paint.

As time passed, the young men began to follow his lead in battle. At the council fires, he spoke wisely and they listened.

Every Ottawa village had many Chiefs, and in time, Pontiac became a respected War Chief.

But far from the blue waters of the Great Lakes, others were at war, too.

For many years, English colonies along the Atlantic coast had been growing and pushing westward. At the same time, the French were building a long chain of forts, from Canada along the Great Lakes—and southward to the Mississippi River.

The English and French were now fighting for control of all the rich lands and waterways of the New World.

At first the English lost one battle after another. They marched in orderly columns to the sound of drums and bagpipes—into bloody ambushes.

But the English sent more and more soldiers. Then Iroquois warriors taught the Redcoats how to fight Indian style.

Slowly, the French chain of forts fell, one by one, into English hands.

16

By the summer of 1760, the French had surrendered Canada and most of their forts in America.

On a cold November day that same year, they gave up Fort Detroit. Indians and French traders gathered outside the walls to watch the Redcoat soldiers march in.

Pontiac's heart was heavy. All his life he had known the friendship of the French. Now, they were leaving.

But there was hope. Neighboring Indians told the Ottawas that English traders gave *more* for their furs. Pontiac listened, but said nothing. Only time would tell what kind of friends these English would be.

Now, the cold winds of winter were upon them. It was time for hunting.

19

The next spring, Pontiac returned to Fort Detroit with his people. The canoes rode low in the water with their heavy loads of furs. The Ottawas were eager to trade.

But the English said they were short of supplies. They gave the Indians no gifts and no food. They demanded three beaver furs for one blanket, and one beaver fur for a pound of gunpowder. The French had always given the powder for nothing.

Most important of all, the English refused to trade much gunpowder.

Pontiac knew that without gunpowder for hunting, his people would go hungry.

He was very angry. These English were not friends.

He knew now that if the thundering cannons of the white men's war came close to the land of the Ottawas, he would help the French.

Pontiac began to travel from tribe to tribe, speaking of the need to join together to fight the English.

In the summer of 1761, the Seneca Indians to the East sent a wampum belt. The beaded belt was a sign for war against the English.

The pattern of the black beads told of English soldiers taking Indian land and giving it to settlers. Soon the Eastern tribes would have no hunting grounds.

The beads called for a surprise attack in early July.

Soon, the war belt had been carried to many tribes. In their villages, Indians made ready for war.

But the surprise did not work. Before many days passed, the English learned all about the Indians' plan. They also knew that there were too few soldiers to fight so many Indians.

Quickly, the English called a council, and invited all the Chiefs of the tribes west of the Alleghenies. At the council, the Englishmen promised that no more Indian land would be taken. They promised to trade fairly. They said they wanted peace.

But Pontiac was not sure that their peace or their promises would last for long.

25

As time passed, the Indians' troubles became worse. In spite of what the English had said, they did not trade enough gunpowder and supplies.

Settlers still continued to move into Ottawa hunting grounds.

Pontiac's anger grew. He often thought of the old days. He wished that the French flag still flew over the fort.

The French had been content to trade, and to send Indian furs across the ocean. But the English had many settlers. They must be stopped!

By now, many tribes had been caught in the war between the French and English. Most were siding with the French.

Secretly, the French were fanning the Indians' desire for war against the English.

Dressed as Indians, some Frenchmen managed to slip past the English-held forts and into the Indian villages.

Pontiac was glad to see his old friends.

His eyes flashed with anger as the French spoke of the English. They used strong words:

"You have no gunpowder because the English plan to kill all Indians. Then they will take your land."

Pontiac listened.

"But our soldiers will return if your tribes fight," the Frenchmen promised. "Together we will drive the English away forever!"

Pontiac's hopes began to rise.

Pontiac sent wampum belts to all the tribes in the Mississippi Valley. Once again, the beads called for war. Quickly, the war belts and hatchets were passed from tribe to tribe.

Pontiac was ready. He called a council to tell the Chiefs of his plan.

By the blazing fire of Pontiac's camp, the Chiefs of the Ottawa, Chippewa, Huron, and Potawatomi Nations listened to the War Chief as he said:

"We must lift the hatchet against the English—now!"

They would wipe out the English. Each tribe would strike the fort nearest its village. Each fort would fall, and then the French would return.

Pontiac himself would lead four tribes. They would drive the English out of Fort Detroit!

But time was against them. Pontiac had no way of knowing that the French would never return . . . that the French had already lost.

The war between England and France had ended in February of 1763. But news traveled very slowly, and it was a long time before any-one—soldiers or Indians—knew of the treaty signed months earlier in Paris.

It was now late April, and Pontiac's war was still in motion.

On May 2nd, Pontiac led three hundred warriors to the gates of Fort Detroit. Under his blanket, each warrior carried a hatchet, a knife, or a musket sawed off at the end so that it could be hidden.

Pontiac's plan was simple. Once his warriors were inside the fort, he would give the signal. They would take the English by surprise!

As soon as they entered the fort, Pontiac knew something was wrong. There were many guards at the gates. Every shop and house was closed tight.

Walking toward the fort's commander, Major Henry Gladwin, Pontiac saw soldiers standing ready to fight. Their bayonets were fixed.

Pontiac knew that to attack now would mean death to many warriors. Someone had warned the English!

His plan had failed. But he was not defeated. He would try again.

When Pontiac returned the next day with his warriors, he had a new trick in mind. He carried a long peace pipe for Major Gladwin.

But the English would only let a few Chiefs in at a time.

When Pontiac returned to his village, he picked up a tomahawk and began to chant a song for war. Then he spoke to his people:

"If we cannot enter the fort, we will surround it and force the English to surrender."

"Soon the French will come to help us, and with them we will drive these English from our lands!"

Pontiac and his men surrounded the fort. Then, day by day, he waited. He was sure the French would come soon. With no food or supplies, the fort would fall easily.

War cries echoed outside the walls of the fort.

36

The Indians set rafts afire and pushed them against any boats that tried to bring in supplies.

Many of the other tribes sent word that they had captured the forts in their areas. Finally, eight English forts had been taken. Yet Fort Detroit still flew the English flag. And there was no sign of help from the French.

By late summer, Pontiac's uprising had spread far to the north and the east. Indians as far away as Pennsylvania, Maryland, and Virginia went on the warpath.

A terrible fear began to grow. In years to come, settlers moving westward would carry this fear with them.

Week after week, Pontiac watched and waited. The French did not come. But a fleet of English ships did!

In late July, twenty-two boats loaded with soldiers, food, and gunpowder managed to reach Fort Detroit. Indian muskets were no match for English cannons!

Pontiac's hope of starving the English into surrender was over.

His own people now had little food. War left no time for hunting. Many tribes were losing their taste for the war. More and more Indians left for their homes. Some of his own Ottawa warriors began to turn away from him.

Rumors came that the English and French had made peace.

But Pontiac refused to believe that the French would never return!

Then, one cold October night, a French trader from Illinois rode into Pontiac's camp.

"Pontiac, my friend," he said, "it is true. My king and the English king have made peace. Now all Chiefs and warriors must bury their hatchets and live with our English brothers."

Pontiac's heart was heavy. The winter snow was beginning to fall. Few friends remained with him.

He sent a short message to the fort. The siege was over.

That winter Pontiac traveled with only his family. Slowly, he made his way to the Illinois Territory. During the long, cold months, he went from tribe to tribe, urging his people to drive out the English.

But in his heart, he knew there was little hope.

The French no longer spoke of helping him. Some were leaving; others would stay and live in peace with the English.

Many of Pontiac's Indian brothers turned their backs on him. His dream was finished.

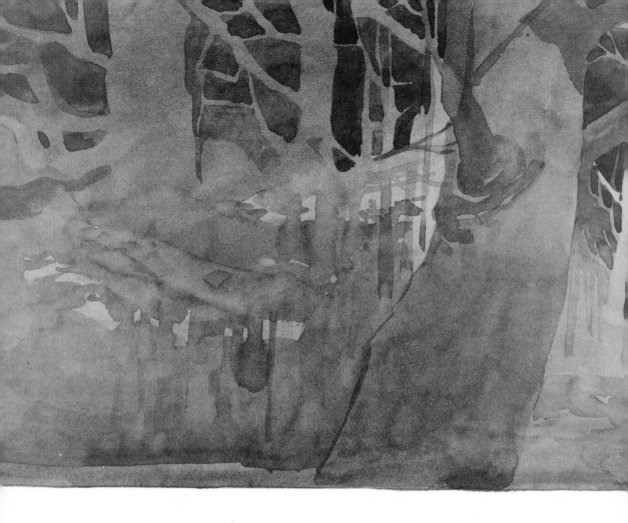

As time passed, more and more English settlers crossed the Alleghenies and came to the rich lands of the Great Lakes. Indians found houses and fences on their hunting grounds.

Secret war belts were still carried from one village to the next. But Pontiac no longer wished to fight. He had seen enough of war.

In August, 1765, Pontiac and thirty other Chiefs signed a treaty of peace at Detroit. There, he asked the English for help for his people.

No longer did they own the vast hunting grounds. They were being pushed off their land; they were hungry. Things would never again be the same.

With his family, Pontiac continued to hunt in the winter, and take his catch to trade in the spring. As the seasons passed, he traveled farther away from his old hunting grounds.

Wherever he went, the news spread quickly. There were many who still feared the once-mighty Chief. There were others who were jealous of the power he had once held.

Late in the spring of 1769, Pontiac brought furs to trade in St. Louis, far from his old home.

It was there that a young Indian brave raised a tomahawk against him and struck him down. Some said that the English had bribed the warrior to kill Pontiac. No one knew for sure.

But one thing was sure. After Pontiac's war, there was no stopping the westward movement of the settlers' wagons.

Never again would the Indians walk peacefully through their hunting grounds. It was the end of the old ways that Pontiac had tried so hard to save.

0632 02 413004 01 6   (IC=1)
FLEISCHER, JANE   12/04/84
PONTIAC, CHIEF OF TH OTTAWAS
(1) 1979 JB PONTIAC

JB   FLEISCHER, JANE

PONT   PONTIAC, CHIEF OF THE

          OTTAWAS

1/81   489

DISCARDED

Harborfields Public Library
Greenlawn, New York
(516) 757 4200

LIBRARY HOURS

Monday thru Thursday	9:00 A.M.-9:00 P.M.
Friday	10:00 A.M.-5:00 P.M.
Saturday	9:00 A.M.-5:00 P.M.
Sunday (Sept. to June)	1:00 P.M.-5:00 P.M.